NATIONAL GEOGRAPHIC LEARNING | **CENGAGE Learning**

Wonderful WORLD 1

PUPIL'S BOOK

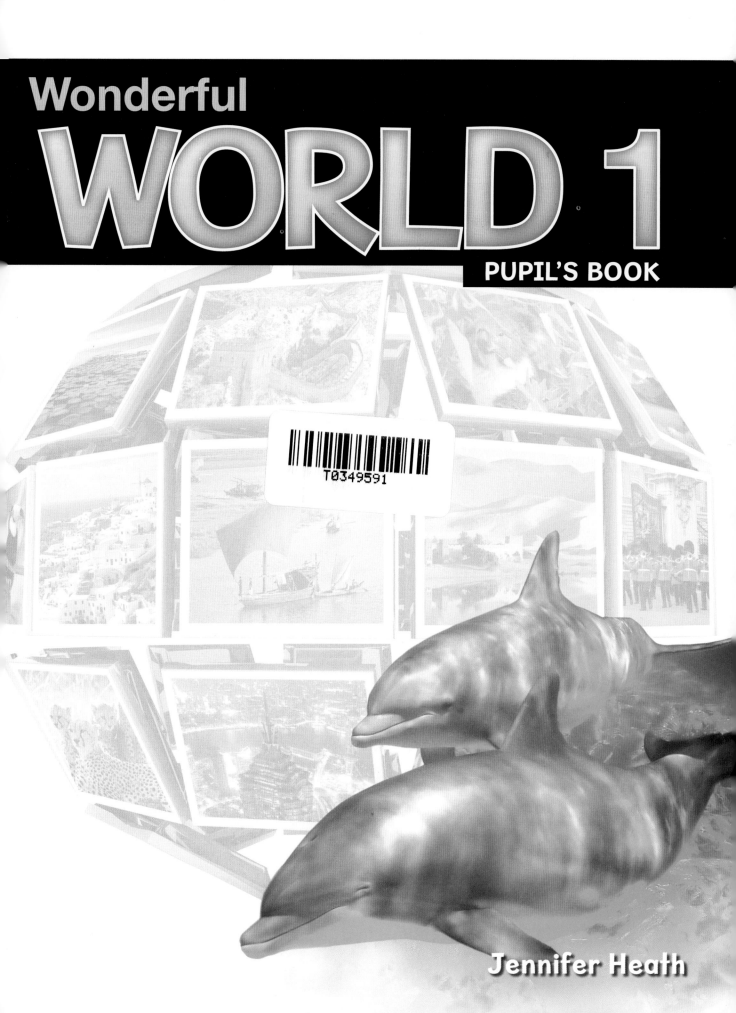

Jennifer Heath

Contents

Alphabet

A **Listen, say and write.**

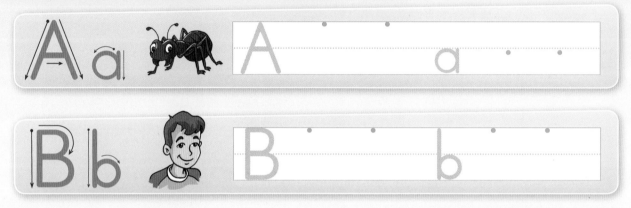

B **Colour A, a, B and b.**

C **Write and find the stickers.**

__nt

__oy

D **Listen and say.**

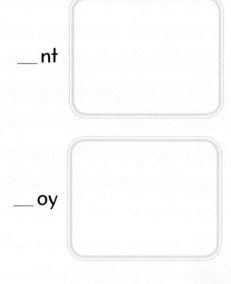

Hi.
My name's Amber.

4

A Listen, say and write.

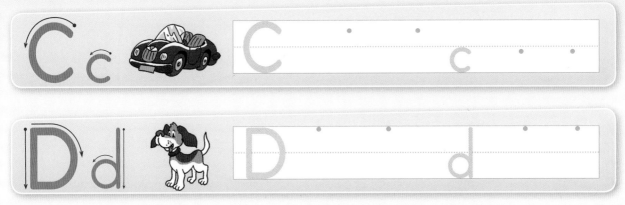

B Circle C, c, D and d.

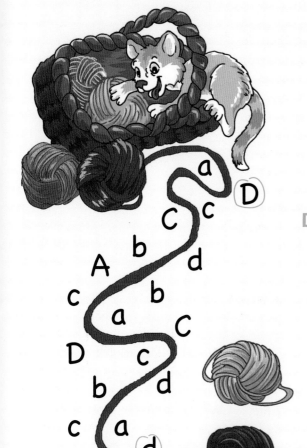

C Write and colour.

__ ar   __ og

D Listen and say.

What's your name?

My name's Chris.

5

Alphabet

E e   F f

A **Listen, say and write.**

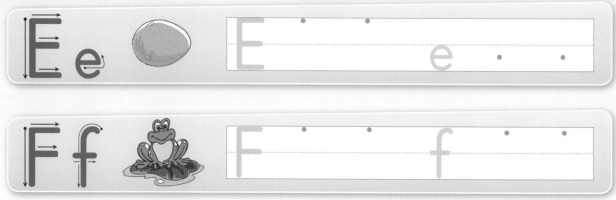

E e   E   e

F f   F   f

B **Join the dots.**

C **Write and find the stickers.**

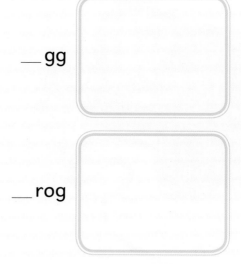

__gg

__rog

D **Chant.**

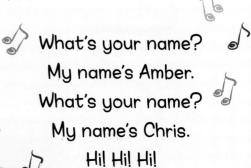

What's your name?
My name's Amber.
What's your name?
My name's Chris.
Hi! Hi! Hi!

G g  H h

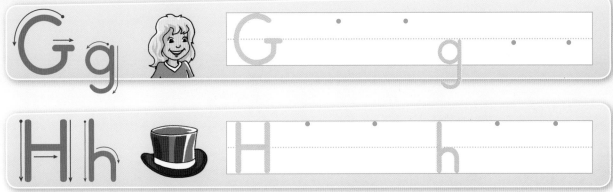

G   g

H   h

B Circle G, g, H and h.

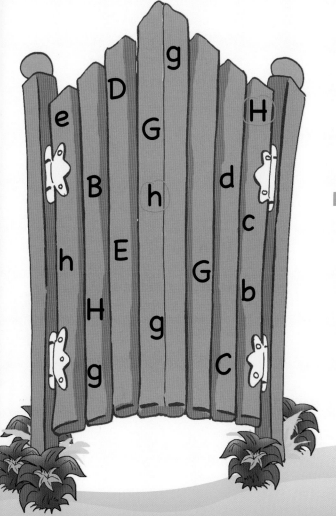

C Write and colour.

__irl   __at

D Listen and say.

Hello. How are you?

Fine, thank you.

7

Alphabet

A **Listen, say and write.**

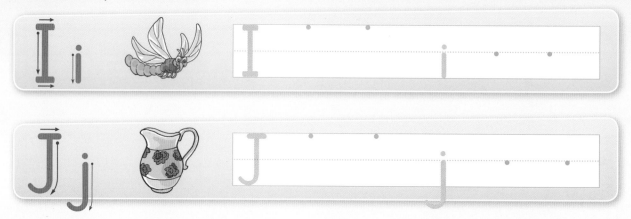

B **Find and circle the letters I, i, J and j.**

C **Write and colour.**

___nsect

___ug

D **Listen and say.**

Hello. My name's Chris. What's your name?

Hi. My name's Amber. How are you?

Fine, thank you.

K k   L l

A **Listen, say and write.**

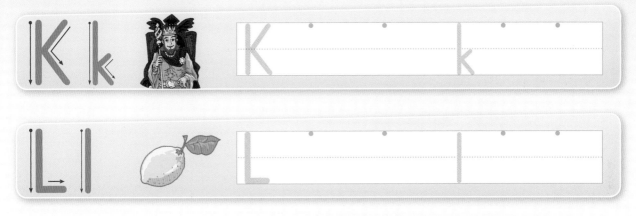

B **Join the dots.**

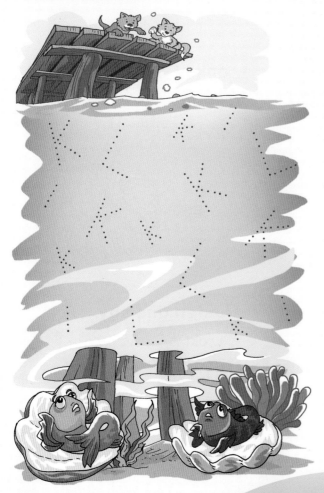

C **Write and find the stickers.**

___ing   ___emon

D **Sing.**

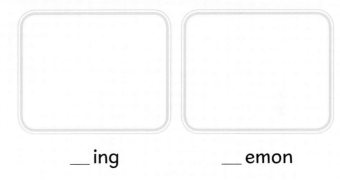

What's your name?
My name's Jane.
How are you?
Fine, thank you.

What's your name?
My name's Joe.
How are you?
Fine, thank you.

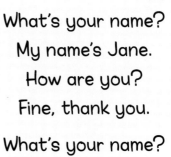

Alphabet

A **Listen, say and write.**

B **Match.**

M

M N

N N

M

m

n

m

n

m n

C **Write and colour.**

__onkey

__est

D **Listen and say.**

Look! An insect.

No! Try again.

A monkey.

Yes! Well done!

O o   P p

A **Listen, say and write.**

B **Colour O, o, P and p.**

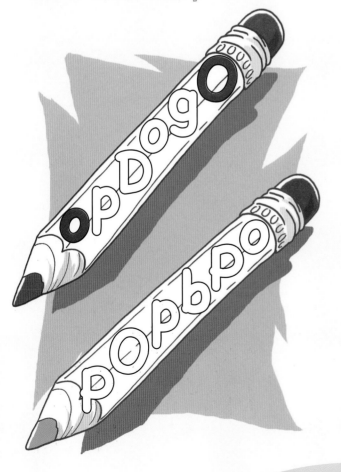

C **Write and find the stickers.**

__ ctopus

__ encil

D **Chant.**

Look! A monkey.
No! Try again!
Look! An octopus.
Yes! Well done!

Alphabet

A **Listen, say and write.**

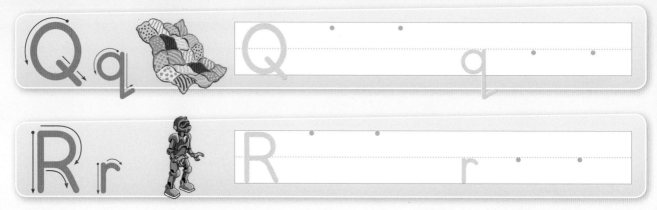

B **Match.**

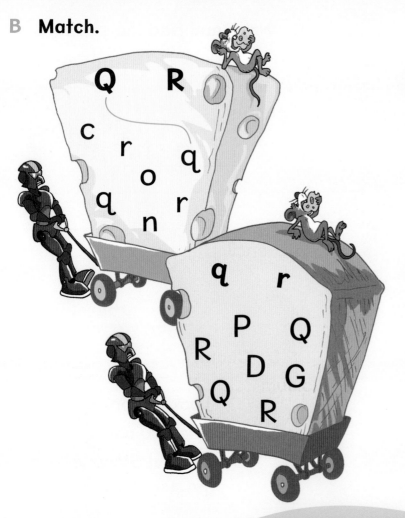

C **Write and colour.**

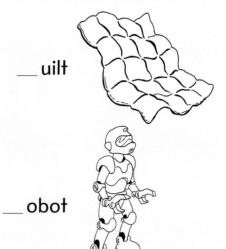

__uilt

__obot

D **Listen and say.**

Here you are.

Wow! Thanks.

You're welcome.

S s   T t

A   Listen, say and write.

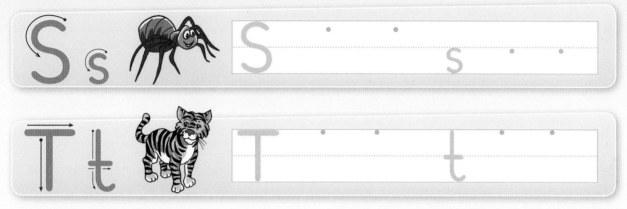

S   s

T   t

B   Colour S, s, T and t.

C   Write and find the stickers.

___ pider

___ iger

D   Chant.

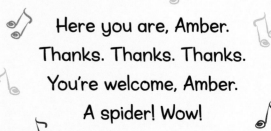

Here you are, Amber.
Thanks. Thanks. Thanks.
You're welcome, Amber.
A spider! Wow!

Alphabet

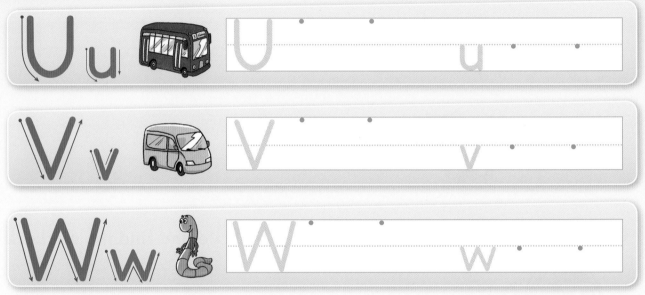

A Listen, say and write.

U u   U   u

V v   V   v

W w   W   w

B Circle U, u, V, v, W and w.

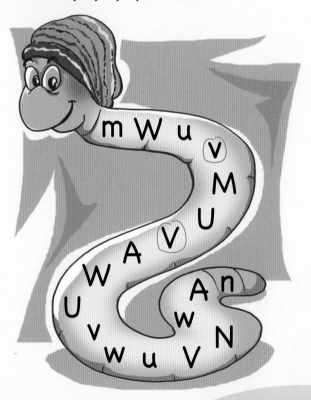

C Write and find the stickers.

b __ s   __ an

__ orm

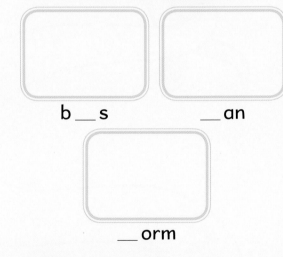

D Listen and say.

Bye, Amber.

Goodbye, Chris.

A Listen, say and write.

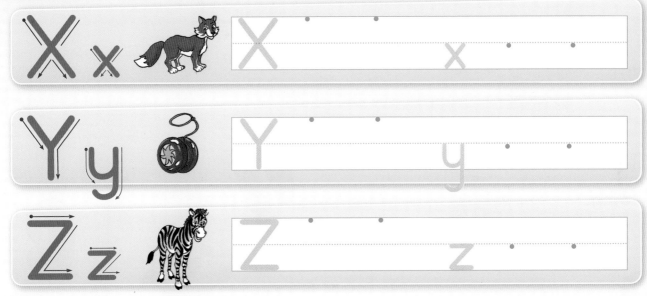

B Find and circle the letters X, x, Y, y, Z and z.

C Write and colour.

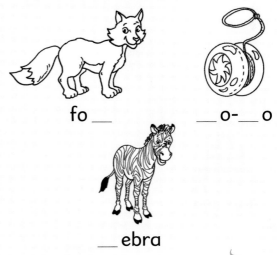

fo __

__o-__o

__ebra

D Sing.

Goodbye, Chris. Bye!

Goodbye, Amber. Bye!

Goodbye! Goodbye!

Bye! Bye!

Alphabet

A Write.

_f _g H_

_c D_ E_

A a B_

I_ J_ K_

_l M_

N_ _o _u _v

_r _s T_ _w

Q_ P_ X_ Y_ Z_

B Sing.

a b c d e f g
a b c d e f g
Sing everybody!
Sing everybody!
Sing the alphabet song!

h i j k l m n
h i j k l m n
Sing everybody!
Sing everybody!
Sing the alphabet song!

o p q r s t u
o p q r s t u
v and w
v and w
X Y Z!

C Play.

D Make.

Colours

A Listen, read and say.

red

blue

pink

brown

black

B Colour and write.

red   pink   brown   black   blue

C Write and match.

1 der   ___red___
2 inkp   _____
3 wronb   _____
4 uebl   _____
5 clabk   _____

D Chant.

Red red red.

Blue blue blue.

Pink pink – Brown brown.

Black black black.

18

E Listen, read and say.

orange

white

purple

yellow

green

F Colour and write.

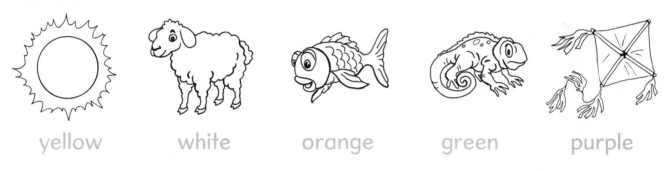

yellow   white   orange   green   purple

G Listen, say and play the game.

Purple. Guess!

A purple van.

No. Try again!

A purple car.

Yes. Well done!

Numbers

A **Listen and say.**

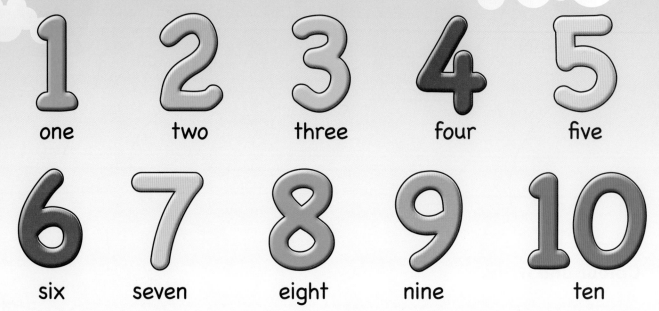

1 one
2 two
3 three
4 four
5 five

6 six
7 seven
8 eight
9 nine
10 ten

B **Find and colour.**

1 blue　　2 purple　　3 pink　　4 brown　　5 yellow
6 green　　7 orange　　8 red　　9 black　　10 white

C **Chant.**

1 2 3
4 5 6
7 8 9
10 10 10!

20

D   Count and write.

1

| 5 | five |

4

| | |

2

| | |

5

| | |

3

| | |

6

| | |

E   Listen and write.

| 2 | | | | |

| | | | | |

F   Listen and say.

How old are you?

I'm nine.

A **Listen and say.**

B Match.

I'm Leo.
My name's Trek.
I'm Ty.
My name's Mia.

 1
 2
 3
 4

C Listen and say.

What's your name?

My name's Chris.

How old are you?

I'm 10.

How are you?

Fine, thanks!

D Colour and write.

Mia   Trek   Leo   Ty

Trek

E Sing.

Happy Trails! Happy Trails!
Hello everybody at
Happy Trails! Happy Trails!
Hello everybody at Happy Trails.

 We're Trek's reporters.
Party! Party! Party!
We're Trek's reporters.
Come on, everybody!

Mia, Ty and Leo too.
Party! Party! Party!
Mia, Ty and Leo too.
Come on, everybody!

23

Africa

baby   fly   elephant   mum   photo   fantastic

A   Listen and read.

1. Look, Trek. A photo and a DVD.
Wow! Africa!

2. Hi Trek! Look! Africa!
Fantastic!

3. Look! An elephant!
Oh yes! A baby!
Oh no! A fly.

4. Look, a baby and mum!
Wow!
Oh no!

5. Oh no!

B Look and learn.

A spider?

No. An octopus.

an ant
a fly

an → a e i o u
a → b c d f g h j k l m n p
       q r s t v w x y z

C Write a or an.

1 _a_ baby   4 ___ girl
2 ___ insect   5 ___ octopus
3 ___ DVD   6 ___ yo-yo

D Listen and tick (✔).

Say it!

Listen and say.
fantastic
elephant

Read and listen.
photo
fly

E Say.

Spell elephant, please.

E-L-E-P-H-A-N-T

Well done!

1 My house is an igloo.

 house   igloo   brother sister   dad   family   cool

A Listen and read.

Jim is a boy. He's seven years old. He's an Inuit!

'My family is cool. Dad is a hunter. He's fantastic! Mum is fantastic too! Amy is my sister. Todd is my brother.

My house is an igloo. It's cool!'

B Write Yes or No.

1 Jim is a girl.   No

2 Jim is eight.   _____

3 Dad is a hunter.   _____

4 An igloo is a house. _____

C Look and learn.

I'm an Inuit.

You're cool!

I'm = I am	I'm a girl.
you're = you are	You are fantastic!
he's = he is	He is a boy.
she's = she is	She's a baby.
it's = it is	It's a house.

D Write am, are or is.

1 He ____is____ a hunter.
2 It _____ a nest.
3 I _____ eight years old.
4 You _____ cool.
5 She _____ a girl.
6 My brother _____ six.

E Sing.

My family is cool.
My family is great.
So come on and celebrate!

Mum is cool.
Dad is cool.
Brothers and sisters.
We're so cool!

1 My family is great.

best friend   grandma grandpa

great
nice

Lesson 3

A Read.

Hi!

My name's Alex. I'm nine years old.

My family is cool. Mum and Dad are from Windsor in England. They're nice. Grandma and Grandpa are great. My brother, Sam, is six. My sister, Lina, is one. She's a baby.

Sue is my friend. We're best friends.

Bye!

Alex

B Circle.

1   Alex is (nine) / six.
2   Sam / Lina is one.
3   Lina is a boy / baby.
4   Alex and Sue are sisters / friends.

30

C Look and learn.

We're cool!

we're = we are
you're = you are
they're = they are

We're nice.
You are friends.
They're sisters.

D Write We're, You're or They're.

1   Sue and I are best friends.   _____We're_____ best friends.
2   Monkeys are nice.   _____ nice.
3   You and Steve are brothers.   _____ brothers.
4   My sister and I are great.   _____ great.

E Say.

Hello. My name's Mary.
I'm seven. I'm from England.

Hi. I'm Rick. I'm eight.
I'm from Africa.

F Draw and write.

Hi! My name's _____ .
I'm _____ years old.
I'm from _____ .

camera   big   small   lion   giraffe   tall   short   funny   Let's go.

A   Listen and read.

B Look and learn.

Look! Two small dogs.

And one big dog!

a boy → boys
a house → houses
a zebra → zebras

C Circle.

1 Look! A (lion) / lions!
2 They're giraffe / giraffes.
3 Wow! It's a camera / cameras.
4 I'm a short girl / girls.
5 We're tall boy / boys.

Say it!

Listen and say.
sister
short

Read and listen.
six
she

D Sing.

Tall or short, big or small,
We're all the same, we're all the same.
Tall or short, big or small,
We're all the same inside.

Boys and girls sing together.
Boys and girls sing together.
Boys and girls sing together.
We're all the same inside.

Boy or girl, mum or dad,
We're all the same, we're all the same.
Boy or girl, mum or dad,
We're all the same inside.

33

2 Toys are fun.

Lesson 2

 ball   computer game   skateboard   toy   fun

A Listen and read.

1

It isn't a dog. It's a robot! It's cool!

A computer game is great! A small game is fun too.

2

3

4

Skateboards are great for boys and girls. But they aren't for a baby. They aren't for grandma or grandpa!

A ball is a nice toy. Balls are small and big. They're for boys, girls, mum and dad — and dogs!

B Match.

1 It's a robot.
2 A small game is fun.
3 A ball is a nice toy.
4 Skateboards aren't for a baby.

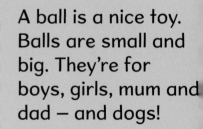

C Look and learn.

I'm not cool!

I'm not = I am not

you aren't = you are not

he isn't = he is not
she isn't = she is not
it isn't = it is not

Rick isn't a nice boy.

we aren't = we are not
you aren't = you are not

they aren't = they are not

They aren't big hats.

D Write 'm not, aren't or isn't.

1 Dad ____isn't____ short.

2 It _____ a great toy.

3 You _____ funny.

4 I _____ a tall boy.

5 Sam and Dan _____ brothers.

E Listen and number.

☐ ☐ ☐ 1 ☐

F Say.

He's a boy. He isn't short. He's tall.

Martin!

2 Happy birthday!

 birthday cake   party   present   teddy bear   happy

A Read.

Happy birthday!

Tina: Happy birthday, Jamie.
Jamie: Thanks.
Tina: Here you are.
Jamie: Wow! A big present! Is it a teddy bear?
Tina: No, it isn't.
Jamie: It's a robot. Cool! Thank you.
Tina: You're welcome. It's a great party. Are you happy?
Jamie: Yes, I am.
Tina: Wow! A big birthday cake.
Jamie: Yes and it's yummy!

B Match.

1 Happy birthday, Jamie.   You're welcome.
2 Is it a teddy bear?   Yes, I am.
3 Thank you.   No, it isn't.
4 Are you happy?   Thanks.

C Look and learn.

Am I ...?	Are we ...?
Yes, I am.	Yes, we are.
No, I'm not.	No, we aren't.
Are you ...?	Are you ...?
Yes, you are.	Yes, you are.
No, you aren't.	No, you aren't.
Is he/she/it ...?	Are they ...?
Yes, he/she/it is.	Yes, they are.
No, he/she/it isn't.	No, they aren't.
Is it nice?	Are you friends?
No, it isn't.	Yes, we are.

D Match.

1 Is it a yellow quilt?   No, he isn't.
2 Are zebras big?   Yes, they are.
3 Am I short?   No, you aren't.
4 Are you ten?   Yes, it is.
5 Is Bill tall?   Yes, we are.

E Say.

F Draw and write.

Wow! _____.

37

bird   whale   mountain   ostrich   penguin   beach

A Listen and read.

My camera! Thanks! This bird is big.

It's an ostrich.

This bird is small!

It's a penguin.

Look. That mountain is big!

This beach is nice. Look! A whale! It's big too.

Goodbye!

Africa is cool!

B Look and learn.

This is a big egg.

That's a big bird! Let's go!

This is a beach.

That is a mountain.

That's = That is

C Write This or That.

That is an ostrich.

1

_____ is a fox.

3

_____ is a cool hat.

2

_____ egg isn't big.

4

Say it!

Listen and say.
beach
camera

Read and listen.
ostrich
octopus

D Listen and write.

1 o _s_ tr _i_ _c_ _h_
2 p ___ ___ gu ___ n
3 ___ ___ e ___ ___ ant
4 ___ h ___ ___ e
5 ___ ir ___ f ___ e

E Say.

This is a worm.

That is a worm.

3 These animals are small.

 lizard   food    hungry   animals   meerkat   snake

A Listen and read.

These animals are meerkats. They are small.

These meerkats are brothers and sisters. They are a family. This meerkat family is big. They are hungry. Spiders, worms, lizards and small snakes are food for meerkats!

B Write Yes or No.

1 Meerkats are small animals.   Yes
2 This family is big.   _____
3 These meerkats are hungry.   _____
4 Big snakes are food for meerkats.   _____

C Look and learn.

These teddy bears are brown.

Those teddy bears are white.

These are meerkats.

Those are spiders.

D Circle.

1 (These) / Those lizards are small.

3 These / Those insects are ants.

2 These / Those igloos aren't big.

4 These / Those mountains are fantastic!

E Sing.

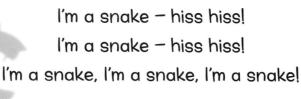

I'm a snake – hiss hiss!
I'm a snake – hiss hiss!
I'm a snake, I'm a snake, I'm a snake!

I'm a lion – roar roar!
I'm a lion – roar roar!
I'm a lion, I'm a lion, I'm a lion!

I'm a penguin – wobble wobble!
I'm a penguin – wobble wobble!
I'm a penguin, I'm a penguin, I'm a penguin!

41

3 What's this?

 dolphin   flower  rabbit  shark   tree

A Read and answer.

This is my Quiz

1

What's this?
a   It's an ostrich.
b   It's a giraffe.

2

What are these?
a   They're penguins.
b   They're rabbits.

3

What's that?
a   It's a beach.
b   It's a mountain.

4

What are those?
a   They're insects.
b   They're birds.

5

What's this?
a   It's a dolphin.
b   It's a shark.

6

What are these?
a   They're trees.
b   They're flowers.

What's your score?   / 6

B Circle.

1

It isn't a shark / dolphin

3

An ostrich is a big bird / insect.

2

A rabbit / giraffe is a tall animal.

4

That flower / tree is small.

42

C Look and learn.

What's this?

It's a bird.

What's this?	It's an octopus.
What's that?	
What are these?	They're whales.
What are those?	
What's = What is	

D Write.

1 What are ____these____ ?

____They're____ nests.

3 What's _____ ?

_____ a ball.

2 What are _____ ?

_____ dolphins.

4 What's _____ ?

_____ a tiger.

E Say.

What's this?

It's a flower.

F Draw and write.

What are these?

_____ .

43

Let's remember!

A Find and stick.

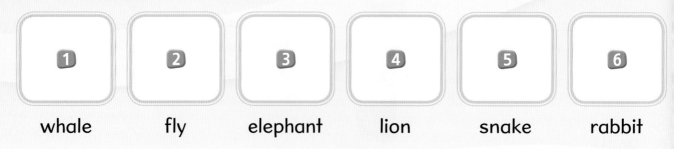

1	2	3	4	5	6
whale	fly	elephant	lion	snake	rabbit

B Write.

C Circle.

1 Giraffes are (tall) / short.

2 Those boys are my brothers / sisters.

3 An ostrich is a big / small bird.

4 Yummy! This birthday camera / cake is nice.

5 Maria is nine. She's my brother / best friend.

6 This robot / lizard is a great toy.

D Write.

am	are	aren't	~~is~~	is	isn't

1 She _____is_____ a cool girl.

2 Are you hungry? Yes, I _____ .

3 Dad _____ a boy!

4 Are they sharks? Yes, they _____ .

5 Look! A beach. It _____ small.

6 Are trees blue? No, they _____ .

E Circle.

1 It's (a) / an house.

2 What's that? It's / They're a spider.

3 Jane and Katy are girl / girls.

4 What are this / these? They're computer games.

5 It's a / an insect.

6 These teddy bear / teddy bears are brown.

F Look and match.

1 What's that?   They're dolphins.

2 Are you a grandma?   No, it isn't.

3 Is it a photo?   It's a mountain.

4 What are those?   Yes, they are.

5 Is this a ball?   No, I'm not.

6 Are they penguins?   Yes, it is.

Fun and Games

Look! It's a birthday party! This is Jenny. She's seven years old. Happy birthday, Jenny!

Quiz time!

What's this?
a It's a birthday cake.
b It's a present.

A Match.

1

2

3

B Sing.

Hi and hello!
Hello and hi!
Boys and girls,
Brothers and sisters,
How are you?

Children of the world,
We're one big family.
Children of the world,
We're one big family.

Hi and hello!
Hello and hi!
Mums and dads,
Grandmas and grandpas,
How are you?

People of the world,
We're one big family.
People of the world,
We're one big family.

C Make.

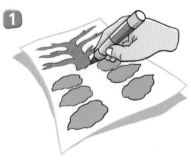

Happy Trails in Australia

Australia

4 Happy Trails in Australia

 drawing helicopter pupil school

numbers 11–20

A Listen and read.

1 Look, Dad! They're in Australia.

They're in a helicopter.

2 There's a great beach.

There's a school.

3 Hi! I'm Mia.

Hello Mia.

How many pupils? Mmm ... eleven!

4 1, 2, 3, 4, 5, 6, 7, 8, 9, 10, 11!

5 Hello, I'm Mr Davis.

There are ... twelve, thirteen, fourteen, fifteen, sixteen ...

6 ... seventeen, eighteen, nineteen, twenty drawings.

B Look and learn.

There are two pupils.

But there's one pencil!

There's a school.
There are twenty drawings.

There's = There is

C Write There's or There are.

1 Look! _____There's_____ a pink house.
2 _____ twelve drawings.
3 _____ three boys in that helicopter.
4 Look! _____ a dog.
5 _____ a bird in that tree.

D Listen and circle.

1 13 / (15)
2 20 / 12
3 5 / 6
4 8 / 18
5 16 / 17

Say it!

Listen and say.
helicopter
flower

Read and listen.
Spider and tiger,
brother and sister.

E Say.

How many teddy bears?

Seven.

Yes. Well done!

51

notebook pen board book computer lesson

A Listen and read.

This is Emma. She's from Alaska. She's a pupil. Emma is at school. This is a lesson.

There are books and notebooks. There are pens and pencils too. There aren't any computers. Is there a board? Yes, there is.

B Write.

1 Emma is a __pupil__ .

2 This is a _____ .

3 There are _____ and notebooks.

4 There aren't any _____ .

5 Is there a _____ ? Yes, there is.

C Look and learn.

Are there any pupils?

No, there aren't.

There isn't a board.
There aren't any pupils.

Is there ...?   Yes, there is. / No, there isn't.
Are there ...?   Yes, there are. / No, there aren't.

Is there a board? Yes, there is.

D Circle.

1 There isn't / There aren't a computer.
2 Are there any books? No, there aren't / isn't.
3 There isn't / There aren't any pens and pencils.
4 There is / There are twenty pupils in this school.
5 Is there / Are there a drawing in the notebook? Yes, there is.

E Sing.

There's a school for you.
There's a school for you.
Is there a school for me?

There are books for you.
There are books for you.
Are there any books for me?

Hooray! Hooray!
Hooray! Hooray!
Let's go to school today!

4 This is my classroom.

Lesson 3

rubber   ruler   desk   chair   apple   classroom   teacher

A Read.

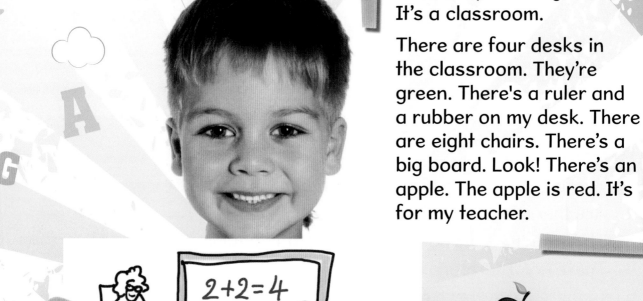

This is my drawing. It's a classroom.

There are four desks in the classroom. They're green. There's a ruler and a rubber on my desk. There are eight chairs. There's a big board. Look! There's an apple. The apple is red. It's for my teacher.

B Circle.

1   The ruler and the rubber are on the chair / desk

2   There are four / eight chairs.

3   The board is small / big.

4   It's a red / green apple.

C Look and learn.

Oh, a dog!

The dog is big!

a ruler
an insect
the desk

There's an apple. The apple is red.
Look! A chair. The chair is big.

D Write a, an or the.

1 Sandra is __a__ pupil.
2 There's a teacher in the classroom. _____ teacher is tall.
3 Look! There's _____ ant on this apple.
4 It's _____ ruler.
5 There's a notebook on that desk. _____ notebook is blue.
6 Look! _____ elephant. The elephant is big.

E Say.

It's a pen.
The pen is green.

F Draw and write.

It's _____.
The _____.

5 Happy Trails in Australia

 eye nose ear kangaroo koala tail long

A Listen and read.

Let's see ...

1
Let's see the animals!
Hooray!

2
What's that?
A tree frog. It's got red eyes.
You've got green eyes.

3
Look! A koala.
It has got a big nose.
Yes, a big black nose!

4
Look! A kangaroo. It's got a long tail.
It's got big ears.
I've got big ears too!
5
I have got a long tail too.

B Look and learn.

This is Chris. He's got a big red nose!

I've got = I have got
you've got = you have got
he's got = he has got
she's got = she has got
it's got = it has got

I've got brown eyes.
She's got a small nose.

C Write have got or has got.

1 A kangaroo _____has got_____ a long tail.
2 My sister _____ a nice nose.
3 I _____ two brothers.
4 Fred _____ small ears.
5 You _____ blue eyes.

Say it!

Listen and say.
tree
green

Read and listen.
Let's see the three trees.

D Chant.

I've got two eyes.
I've got two ears.
I've got a mouth and nose.
Hey, boys and girls
Come and see!
I've got a big tail too!

Do the kangaroo hop!
Let's do the kangaroo hop!
Come on everybody.
Jump up and down!
Do the kangaroo hop!

 hair  arm finger leg toe sad  wet

A Listen and read.

'We are tall. We are short. We've got brown hair and black hair.'

These girls are happy. They aren't sad. They are wet! They've got wet arms and wet legs! They've got wet fingers and wet toes too!

B Write Yes or No.

1 The girls are sad. _No_
2 They are wet. _____
3 They've got wet toes too. _____
4 They've got red hair. _____

58

C Look and learn.

We've got green hair!

we've got = we have got
you've got = you have got
they've got = they have got

They've got ten fingers.

D Write.

1 we / wet hair

 We've got wet hair.

2 you / ten toes

 _____

3 John and Christie / red hair

 _____

4 Sammy and I / blue eyes

 _____

E Listen and write.

| blue | ~~brown~~ | green | long | red | short |

Name	Eyes	Hair
Jane	brown	
Greg		
Eric and Ann		

F Say.

I'm tall. I've got short hair and blue eyes.

5 My cat is fat.

 cat fish parrot  pet fat thin

A Read.

1

> I'm Lars and this is my sister, Anna. I haven't got a brother.

2

> I'm Maria. This is my cat. I'm thin. My cat is fat!

3

> I'm Denzel. This is my brother, Tom. We've got black hair and brown eyes. We haven't got a pet.

4

> I'm Lynn. I've got a fish and a parrot. My parrot has got two legs and a tail. My fish hasn't got legs, but it's got a tail.

B Match.

 1

 2

 3

 4

I've got a fish and a parrot.

I'm thin.

We haven't got a pet.

I haven't got a brother.

C Look and learn.

I haven't got a brother. I've got a friend.

I haven't got	we haven't got
you haven't got	you haven't got
he hasn't got	
she hasn't got	they haven't got
it hasn't got	

haven't = have not
hasn't = has not

It hasn't got big ears.   We haven't got a dog.

D Circle.

1 I haven't got / hasn't got a koala.
2 She have / has not got a thin cat.
3 Boys and girls have / has not got tails!
4 George haven't got / hasn't got a rabbit.
5 You have / has not got a bird.

E Say.

This is my pet. It's fat. It's got a nice tail. It hasn't got arms and legs.

F Draw and write.

This is my pet. It's _____.
It's got _____.
It hasn't got _____.

mask   flippers   mobile phone   bag   map

beautiful
Come on!

A   Listen and read.

1. Goodbye. — Bye!

2. Have you got the map, Ty? — Yes, I have.

3. Have we got the masks? — Yes, we have. They're in that bag. — I've got my mask, my flippers and my camera. Come on!

4. Wow! It's fantastic! — Those fish are beautiful! Oh! An octopus!

5. It's my mobile phone. It's Mr Davis! He says goodbye!

6. Bye! — Australia is great!

B Look and learn.

Have you got my mask and my flippers?

No, I haven't.

Have I got ...?
Yes, I have.
No, I haven't.

Have you got ...?
Yes, you have.
No, you haven't.

Has he/she/it got ...?
Yes, he/she/it has.
No, he/she/it hasn't.

Has it got legs?
Yes, it has.

Have we got ...?
Yes, we have.
No, we haven't.

Have you got ...?
Yes, you have.
No, you haven't.

Have they got ...?
Yes, they have.
No, they haven't.

Have they got maps?
No, they haven't.

C Write.

1 Have dogs got fingers?   No, they ___haven't___ .
2 Have you got a mobile phone?   Yes, I _____ .
3 Has a fish got a tail?   Yes, it _____ .
4 Have you got flippers?   No, we _____ .
5 Has Emily got a nice bag?   Yes, she _____ .

D Listen and write P (Paul) or J (Jane).

1 map   [P]
2 flippers   [ ]
3 masks   [ ]
4 camera   [ ]
5 mobile phone [ ]

E Say.

Have you got flippers?

Yes, I have.

No, I haven't. Have you got a mask?

63

jacket shirt shoes skirt socks clothes dancer

A **Listen and read.**

Fiona is from Scotland. She's nine years old and she's a dancer.

Fiona's clothes are nice. The skirt is red and black. Fiona's socks are red and black too. They're long. The jacket is black and the shoes are black too. Fiona's shirt is white. Look at Fiona's hat. It's cool!

B **Circle.**

1 Fiona's skirt is white / (red) and black.
2 Fiona's socks are long / short.
3 The shirt / jacket is black.
4 Fiona has got / hasn't got a hat.

C Look and learn.

Amber's clothes are beautiful.

The girl's hat is green.
Mum's shoes are red.

D Write

1 the dog / toy

   It's the dog's toy.

2 Bert / shirt

   _____

3 Mum / hat

   _____

4 Izzy / jacket

   _____

E Sing.

Crazy hats, crazy hats!
We've got crazy hats!
Big hats.
Small hats.
We've got crazy hats!

Funny socks, funny socks!
We've got funny socks!
Long socks.
Short socks.
We've got funny socks!

Cool shoes, cool shoes!
We've got cool shoes!
Big shoes.
Funny shoes.
We've got cool shoes!

6 My clothes are cool.

Lesson 3

scarf   T-shirt   boots   dress   jeans   new

A   Read.

Let's play.

Mark:	Come on. Let's play, Kitty!
Kitty:	No. My dress is new.
Mark:	Your dress is funny!
Kitty:	No, it isn't. It's beautiful. Your jeans and T-shirt are funny!
Mark:	No, they aren't! My clothes are cool.
Kitty:	Pink clothes are cool.
Mark:	Pink is for girls! Blue is for boys!
Kitty:	Dad has got a pink scarf.
Mark:	No, he hasn't.
Kitty:	Yes, he has. And Mum has got blue boots!

B   Write.

1 Kitty's ____dress____ is new.

2 Mark's _____ and T-shirt are funny.

3 Blue is for _____ .

4 Dad has got a pink _____ .

5 Mum has got blue _____ .

66

C Look and learn.

Your scarf is great!

Thanks!

my	
your	our
his	your
her	their
its	

Her dress is nice.
Our jeans are orange!

D Write.

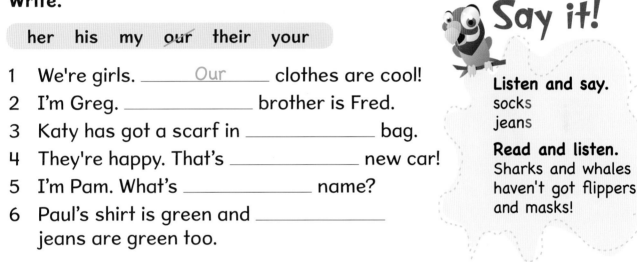

her   his   my   ~~our~~   their   your

1 We're girls. _____Our_____ clothes are cool!
2 I'm Greg. _____ brother is Fred.
3 Katy has got a scarf in _____ bag.
4 They're happy. That's _____ new car!
5 I'm Pam. What's _____ name?
6 Paul's shirt is green and _____ jeans are green too.

Say it!

Listen and say.
socks
jeans

Read and listen.
Sharks and whales haven't got flippers and masks!

E Say.

My jeans are red.
My shoes are black.
My T-shirt is white.
I'm cool!

F Draw and write.

My _____ .
My _____ .
My _____ .
I'm cool!

Let's remember!

A Find and stick.

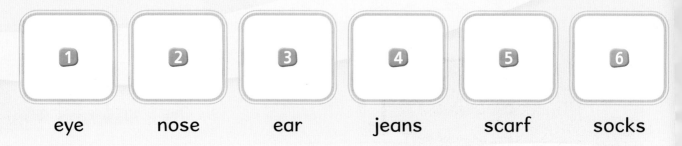

| 1 | 2 | 3 | 4 | 5 | 6 |

| eye | nose | ear | jeans | scarf | socks |

B Write.

board   desk   dress   ~~jacket~~   skirt   ruler

Clothes	Classroom
jacket	

C Circle.

1 Dogs have got four (legs) / ears.
2 There are two pens / pupils in my bag.
3 Have you got long chair / hair?
4 I've got a pet fish / map.
5 His cat has got a long toe / tail.
6 My drawing is in my ruler / notebook.

D Write 've got, haven't got, 's got or hasn't got.

 **1**  **2**  **3**

 **4**  **5**  **6**

1 She ____'s got____ a red apple.

2 It _____ twelve fingers.

3 They _____ new flippers and masks.

4 He _____ a blue shirt.

5 I _____ red shoes.

6 We _____ a mobile phone.

E Write.

1 rubber / a / on / there's / chair / the
    There's a rubber on the chair.

2 bag / aren't / pencils / fifteen / in / there / my
    _____

3 ? / helicopters / any / there / are
    _____

4 T-shirt / green / got / a / I've
    _____

5 ? / he / has / got / parrots / two
    _____

F Circle.

1 Look! A book. A /(The)book is pink.

2 Mum's / Mum dress is long.

3 John is ten. His / Her sister is six.

4 I've got an / a present for my teacher.

5 We're thin. Their / Our friends are thin too.

6 The boy's / boys shoes are wet.

69

Quiz time!

How many legs has a spider got?
a eight
b six

This boy is from Morocco. His name is Tamir. He's cool!

A **Colour.**

B **Sing.**

I've got big eyes.
Big eyes! Big eyes!
I've got a red nose.
Red nose! Red nose!
Wiggle your fingers.
Wiggle wiggle wiggle!
Come on, kids! Let's play!

I'm funny Freddy.
I'm funny Freddy.
Wiggle wiggle wiggle!
Let's play today!
I'm funny Freddy.
I'm funny Freddy.
Wiggle wiggle wiggle!
Hooray! Hooray!

C **Make.**

71

Happy Trails in Brazil

Brazil

7 Happy Trails in Brazil

 swim  sea  look at run play volleyball jump

very
everybody

A Listen and read.

B Look and learn.

I can jump.

I can't jump.

I/you/he/she/it/we/you/they **can**
I/you/he/she/it/we/you/they **can't**

can't = cannot

We can run.
He can't play volleyball.

C Write **can** or **can't**.

1  I ___can___ jump.

2  A snake _____ run.

3  Dogs _____ swim.

4  Mark _____ play beach volleyball.

 **Say it!**

Listen and say.
can
can't

Read and listen.
Elephants can run,
but they can't jump.

D Sing.

Dance everybody! We can dance.
Dance everybody! We can dance.

Sit down, stand up.
We can clap our hands!
Sit down, stand up.
We can clap our hands!

Jump left, jump right.
You can clap your hands!
Jump left, jump right.
You can clap your hands!

75

guitar · recorder · drums · piano · music · sing

What a noise!

A Listen and read.

This school is in Japan. Mrs Chan is a music teacher. Can she play the piano? Yes, she can. She can play the recorder and the guitar too. But she can't play the drums.

Oh no! Look at those boys! Their names are Lee and Kim. Can they sing? No, they can't. Lee's fingers are in his ears! What a noise!

B Circle.

1 (Mrs) / Mr Chan is a music teacher.

2 She can play the guitar / drums.

3 Lee and Kim can / can't sing.

4 Lee's fingers / toes are in his ears.

C Look and learn.

Can you play the guitar, Amber?

No, I can't.

Can I/you/he/she/it/we/you/they ...?
Yes, I/you/he/she/it/we/you/they can.
No, I/you/he/she/it/we/you/they can't.

Can he sing? Yes, he can.
Can they play the drums? No, they can't.

D Write.

1 Can a shark swim? _____ Yes, it can.
2 Can you sing? _____
3 Can your best friend play a recorder? _____
4 Can frogs jump? _____
5 Can you and your friend play volleyball? _____
6 Can a worm run? _____

E Listen and number.

☐   ☐ 1   ☐   ☐   ☐

F Say.

This is my best friend. His name is Mike. He can swim. He can't play the piano.

7 This is my drawing.

Lesson 3

 listen to   read ride a bike  watch TV

song
Guess what!

A Read.

I'm Simon. This is my drawing. It's my family. Grandpa is reading a book. Mum is listening to music. Dad is watching TV. My sister, Helen, is riding a bike. Grandma is singing a song.

Look at the boy! That's me! Guess what! I'm watching TV too!

B Match.

1   He is reading a book.
2   She is listening to music.
3   He is watching TV.
4   She is riding a bike.
5   She is singing a song.
6   I'm watching TV.

78

C Look and learn.

I'm running.

I'm watching.

I'm playing = I am playing
you're playing = you are playing
he's playing = he is playing
she's playing = she is playing
it's playing = it is playing

ride = riding
run = running
swim = swimming

John is singing.

D Write.

1   I ___'m listening___ (listen) to music.

2   Kate _____ (ride) her bike.

3   It _____ (swim).

4   You _____ (run).

E Say.

She's reading a book.
He's playing the drums.

F Draw and write.

Mum is _____.

Dad _____.

I _____.

baseball   football   basketball   tennis   think   win

Lesson 1

A   Listen and read.

1 We're thinking.

2 Baseball is great.
Tennis is cool.
Basketball is nice.

3 Hey! This is Brazil. Come on!

Football! Well done Mia!

Look. It's Brazil. They are winning.

5 Hooray! It's 2–1.

Football is fantastic!

6 Look! The Amazon.

Cool!

Let's go to the Amazon!

B Look and learn.

We're playing basketball!

we're singing = we are singing
you're singing = you are singing
they're singing = they are singing

They are jumping.

C Circle.

1 We is /(are) playing beach volleyball.
2 They are win / winning.
3 We're / We riding our bikes.
4 You are / is running on the beach.
5 They're / They watching TV.
6 We're playing / play the piano.

D Listen and match.

What are they playing?

1 Sandra   2 Adam

3 Tim and Paula   4 John

5 Katy

basketball   volleyball

football   tennis   baseball

E Say.

We're running.

8 They're having fun.

 old
 people
 rollercoaster
 town
 sit stand

A Listen and read.

have fun

This is Blackpool. It's a very old town in England. There's a rollercoaster in Blackpool. It's new. Its name is The Big One. It's very, very big!

Look at these people. They're riding the rollercoaster. They aren't standing. They're sitting. They're having fun!

B Write Yes or No.

1 Blackpool is a new town.   No

2 There's a rollercoaster in Blackpool.   _____

3 The rollercoaster is very small.   _____

4 The people are sitting in the rollercoaster.   _____

5 They're having fun.   _____

C Look and learn.

Amber isn't having fun!

I'm not playing	we aren't playing
I am not playing	we are not playing
you aren't playing	you aren't playing
you are not playing	you are not playing
he/she/it isn't playing	they aren't playing
he/she/it is not playing	they are not playing

I'm not sitting on the chair.
They aren't watching TV.

D Write.

1 Sandy ___isn't riding___ (not ride) the rollercoaster.
2 You _____ (not swim).
3 I _____ (not watch) a DVD.
4 We _____ (not listen) to music.
5 George _____ (not stand).

Say it!

Listen and say.
happy
Yes!

Read and listen.
A very big funny yellow yo-yo!

E Sing.

Rollercoasters are great.
Rollercoasters are cool.
Come on, everybody.
Let's have some fun!

Up, up, up we go.
Look at us.
Down, down, down we go.
Look at us.

We are riding the rollercoaster.
We are having fun.
Come on, everybody.
Put your hands up.
Rollercoasters are fun!

83

8 Are they playing?

climb   cook   dance   kick   rock

A   Read.

1

What's that? Is it a mountain? No it isn't. It's a big rock. Look! There's Tina and Lori. They're climbing the rock.

2

This is Ann. It's her birthday party. Is she dancing? No, she isn't. She's standing.

3

Look at Sam. He's playing football. Is he kicking the ball? Yes, he is.

4

I'm Luke and this is my sister Cindy. Are we cooking? No, we aren't. We're playing. What a noise!

B   Match.

1   Tina and Lori are   playing.
2   Ann is   standing.
3   Luke and Cindy are   climbing a rock.
4   Sam is   kicking the ball.

84

C Look and learn.

Are you winning?

Yes, I am.

Am I playing?	Are we playing?
Yes, I am.	Yes, we are.
No, I'm not.	No, we aren't.
Are you playing?	Are you playing?
Yes, you are.	Yes, you are.
No, you aren't.	No, you aren't.
Is he/she/it playing?	Are they playing?
Yes, he/she/it is?	Yes, they are.
No, he/she/it isn't.	No, they aren't.
Is it jumping?	Are they reading?
Yes, it is.	No, they aren't.

D Write.

1 Are the boys playing football?   Yes, _they are_ .
2 Are you and Dad sitting?   No, _____ .
3 Is the cat running?   No, _____ .
4 Is the girl riding a bike?   Yes, _____ .
5 Is Grandpa playing tennis?   No, _____ .

E Say.

Are you climbing?

Yes, we are.

F Draw and write.

My friends are _____ .
They aren't _____ .

 boat  cinema theatre   market city

Be careful!

A Listen and read.

1. Wow! The Amazon!
   Look! There's a city.

2. Is that a cinema?
   No, it isn't. It's a theatre.

3. This is a great market.
   Ahhh!
   Be careful, Ty!

4. What are you doing?
   We're standing in a boat.
   Come on, Mia!

5. The Amazon is very big!

6. Brazil is great!

B Look and learn.

What are you doing?

I'm watching TV.

What am I doing?
What are you/we/they doing?
What's he/she/it doing?

What's = What is

What's he doing?
He's swimming.

C Write.

1 What <u>are you</u> doing? I am thinking.
2 What _____ doing? He's running.
3 What _____ doing? She's playing.
4 What _____ doing? They're cooking.
5 What _____ doing? We're reading.

Say it!

Listen and say.
theatre
there

Read and listen.
There are three theatres in this town.

D Listen and tick (✔).

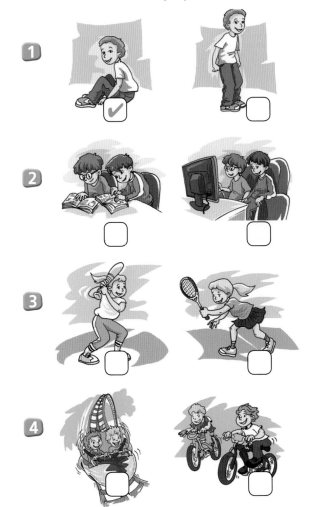

1

2

3

4

F Say.

What are you doing?

I'm reading.

9 It's New Year!

Lesson 2

 colours dragon fireworks sky

New Year

A Listen and read.

This is a Chinese dragon. It's beautiful. Look at the colours. The dragon is dancing. Music is playing. Everybody is happy. It's New Year!

New Year in China is great. There are dragons and fireworks in the sky.

B Write.

1 The ___dragon___ is dancing.
2 _____ is playing.
3 Everybody is _____ .
4 _____ in China is great.
5 There are dragons and _____ in the sky.

C Look and learn.

Dance, Amber!

Don't run, Chris!

Jump!
Don't **jump**!

D Circle.

1 Sit / Don't sit on the chair.

3 Dance / Don't dance **everybody!**

2 Swim / Don't swim **in the sea!**

4 Look / Don't look **at the fireworks.**

E Sing.

Fireworks in the sky!
Whizz! Pop! Whoosh!
Red and blue, yellow and green.
Whizz! Pop! Whoosh!

It's New Year today.
Hooray! Hooray! Hooray!
It's New Year today.
Hooray! Hooray! Hooray!

9 Let's go to London!

 buy   park

 picnic

 river

 shop

lots of ride thing

A Read.

London

**Let's go to London! It's a big city.
What can we see? Lots of things!**

Let's see the city.
Let's go on a bus ride!

There are lots of shops!
Let's buy presents!

The parks are beautiful.
Let's have a picnic!

The river is very long.
Let's go on a boat ride!

There are great markets!
There are theatres and cinemas too!

Look at our poster!

B Circle.

1 London is a big (city) / town.
2 You can buy presents in the shops / theatres.
3 Let's have a bus ride / picnic.
4 The river is very short / long.
5 Let's have / go on a boat ride.

C Look and learn.

Let's go on a bus ride!

OK!

Let's go to the shops!
Let's buy a map!

D Write.

1 London / go / to / let's

 Let's go to London!

2 let's / picnic / a / have

_____

3 theatre / let's / to / the / go

_____

4 the / see / let's / fireworks

_____

E Say.

Let's go to the park!

Let's go to the theatre!

F Draw and write.

My City!
Let's go to _____.
There are lots of _____.
There is a _____ too.

Let's remember!

A Find and stick.

1	2	3	4	5	6
rock	boat	park	river	rollercoaster	city

B Write.

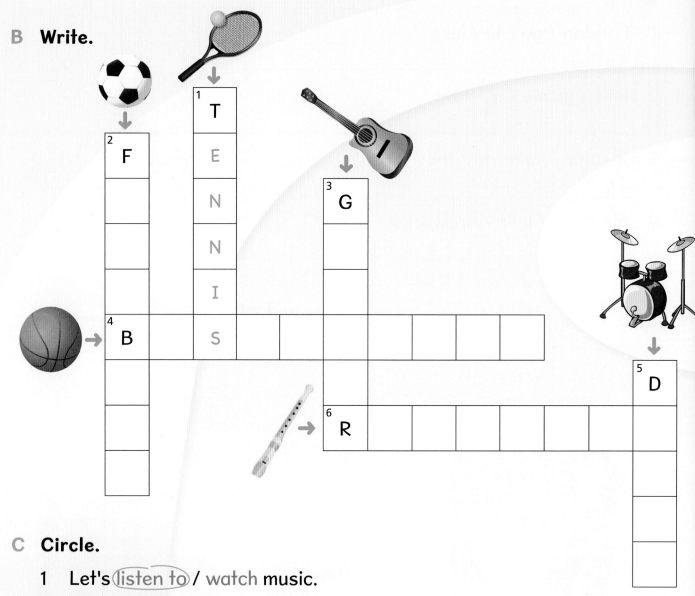

C Circle.

1 Let's listen to / watch music.
2 Can you play the cinema / piano?
3 Dad is reading / riding a book.
4 The sea is nice. Let's swim / stand.
5 We're buying apples at the theatre / market.
6 My brother can climb / jump mountains.

92

D Circle.

1 I'm (watching) / watch TV.

2 Are / Is he cooking?

3 Are they thinking? No, they are / aren't.

4 She isn't / aren't playing baseball.

5 I 'm not / aren't singing.

6 What are you doing? I'm playing / doing computer games.

E Write can or can't.

1 Dogs ____can't____ climb a tree.

2 Elephants _____ ride a bike.

3 These cakes are yummy. You _____ cook.

4 Can your brother sing? Yes, he _____ .

5 Can frogs run? No, they _____ .

6 I'm very tall. I _____ play basketball.

F Write.

| Dance   Don't   Don't   Let's   Let's   Look |

1 This party is great! ____Let's____ have fun!

2 _____ play football in the house! Go to the park!

3 There's the river. _____ go for a boat ride.

4 _____ at the fireworks in the sky! They're beautiful.

5 The music is fantastic. _____ everybody!

6 Tommy! _____ kick your sister!

Fun & Games

My name is Kay. I'm having fun! I'm riding my bike in the park.

Quiz time!

Is there a bike for two people?
a Yes, there is.
b No, there isn't.

A Find.

B Sing.

I'm riding a bike.
I'm riding a bike.
I'm riding a bike,
    In the park.

I'm kicking a ball.
I'm kicking a ball.
I'm kicking a ball,
    In the park.

I'm singing a song.
I'm singing a song.
I'm singing a song,
    In the park.

We're having fun!
We're having fun!
We're having fun,
    In the park!

C Make.

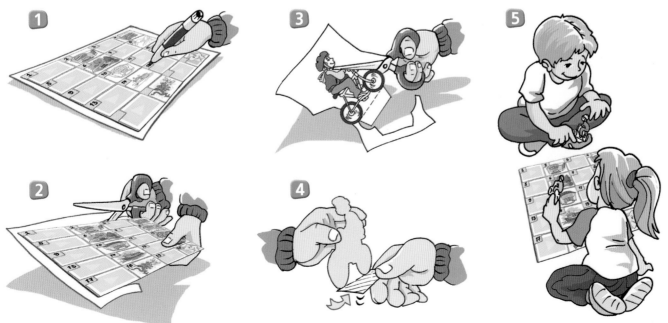

95

Happy Trails in Greece

Greece

 glass bedroom living room kitchen man reporter

I'm sorry.
Welcome to ...

A Listen and read.

1 What are you doing?

I'm watching a DVD. Look at those men, Tessy.

2 Hello! I'm Mr Nikou. Are you Trek's reporters?

Yes, we are. I'm Mia.

I'm Leo.

He's a very tall man!

3 Hi. I'm Ty. What's your name?

My name's George. Let's go to my house!

4 This is my mum. The babies are my sisters.

Hello, Mrs Nikou.

Hi.

Your living room is nice.

5 This is my bedroom.

Oh no! I'm sorry, Leo.

Come to the kitchen!

6 Have you got glasses?

Yes, we have.

Welcome to Greece!

B Look and learn.

Those men are tall.

Those women are short!

a baby → babies
a bus → buses
a glass → glasses
a fox → foxes
a beach → beaches
a tomato → tomatoes

Look!

a man → men
a woman → women
a child → children
a foot → feet

C Write.

1 _____ostrich_____    _____ostriches_____

2 _____   _____

3  _____   _____

4  _____    _____

5 _____    _____

D Listen and circle.

1 Mrs Nikou is in the (kitchen) / bedroom.

2 Mr Nikou is in the bedroom / living room.

3 George is in the living room / bedroom.

4 The babies are in the kitchen / living room.

5 Leo is in the living room / kitchen.

E Say.

This is my house. It's got a big kitchen. It's got a beautiful living room. There are two bedrooms and they're small.

10 Sandy is making cakes.

butter   chocolate   flour   milk   face   make

A Listen and read.

This is Sandy. She's six years old. She's making some cakes. She's having fun!

There are twelve cakes. They're yummy! Look! Sandy's got chocolate on her face. It's on her fingers too!

You can make these cakes with some milk and lots of chocolate. Is there any flour and butter in these cakes? Yes, there is. There are some eggs too.

B   Write Yes or No.

1   Sandy is having fun.   Yes

2   There are six cakes.   _____

3   There's chocolate on Sandy's face and fingers.   _____

4   The cakes have got flour and butter.   _____

5   There are some eggs in the cakes.   _____

C Look and learn.

Have we got any eggs?

No, we haven't got any eggs now!

I've got some apples.
He's got some chocolate.

I haven't got any apples.
He hasn't got any chocolate.

Have I got any apples?
Has he got any chocolate.

D Write some or any.

1 I haven't got _____any_____ flour.
2 There's _____ milk in the kitchen.
3 Dad is buying _____ books.
4 Have you got _____ computer games?
5 You've got _____ chocolate on your nose!
6 Have we got _____ butter, Mum?

E Sing.

Rub your tummy.
Rub your tummy.
Milk and chocolate today!

Rub your tummy.
Rub your tummy.
Milk and cakes today!

Yummy, yummy, yummy!
Come on rub your tummy!
Yummy, yummy, yummy!

10 Where are the oranges?

Lesson 3

basket   carrot   cheese   orange   potato   sweets

A Read.

Wendy: Let's buy some potatoes, Mum.
         They're next to the carrots.

Mum: OK, Wendy. We haven't got any eggs. Can you
         see the eggs?

Wendy: Yes, they're behind the tomatoes.

Mum: Let's buy some apples too.

Wendy: OK. Let's see ... milk. Where's the milk?

Mum: It's in front of the cheese.

Wendy: Have we got any oranges?

Mum: Yes, we have. Look. They're in the basket.
         They're under the eggs.

Wendy: Great. Where are the sweets?

Mum: No sweets, Wendy!

Wendy: Come on, Mum. Please!

Mum: No, Wendy! I'm sorry. Let's go.

potatoes
eggs
apples
milk
oranges

B Write.

1   The potatoes are next to the _____carrots_____ .
2   The _____ are behind the tomatoes.
3   The milk is in front of the _____ .
4   The oranges are in the _____ .

C Look and learn.

Where are the sweets?

They're in my tummy!

Where's the glass?
Where are the glasses?
Where's = Where is

in   on

in front of   behind

next to   under

D Circle

1 Mr Terry is (in) / on the car.

2 Ann is in front of / behind John.

3 Mark is on / under his desk.

4 Dad is next to / in front of the bike.

Say it!

Listen and say.
Wendy
sweets

Read and listen.
Where are Wendy's twenty sweets?

E Say.

The cheese is next to the basket.

The oranges are in the basket.

F Draw and write.

My shopping basket.
The _____ .
The _____ .
The _____ .

love   work

Sunday   Thursday
Monday   Friday
Tuesday   Saturday
Wednesday

Lesson 1

A Listen and read.

1

Hooray! It's Saturday!

2

Hello!

Hello, Mr Nikou. Hi, George!

Let's go!

3

On Saturday I go to my grandma's house.

On Friday I work, but I have fun on Saturday and Sunday!

4

George! I love you!

OK, OK Grandma! I love you too!

5

I cook on Monday and Tuesday.

And Wednesday and Thursday and Friday!

Yummy! Your grandma makes great cakes.

6

I'm happy. I love my boy!

OK, OK Mum! I love you too!

B Look and learn.

C Circle.

1 I (love) / loves Grandpa.
2 You goes / go to the market on Monday.
3 On Wednesday Kelly rides / ride her bike.
4 My cat climb / climbs trees.
5 Roy play / plays the guitar.
6 I buy / buys sweets on Saturday.

Say it!

Listen and say.
George
great

Read and listen.
George the dragon
is great friends with
Gabby the giraffe.

D Sing.

Monday is OK.
Tuesday is OK.
Wednesday is good,
I say!

Thursday is OK.
Friday is OK.
All the days are good,
I say.

But Saturday is great,
And Sunday is fantastic.
They're the best days,
I say!

Saturday and Sunday.
Saturday and Sunday.
I love Saturday and Sunday!

11 We love snow.

 snow castle breakfast eat get up wear

A Listen and read.

These children are in a park. They've got a big snow castle!

On Saturday they get up. They eat breakfast. They wear lots of clothes and they go to the park. The park is in front of their school. They play on the snow castle. Their mums and dads play too.

'We love the snow castle. We play and we have fun.'

B Match.

1. They get up.
2. They eat breakfast.
3. They wear lots of clothes.
4. They play on the snow castle.

C Look and learn.

We love snow.

We eat snow!

we read
you read
they read

On Saturday they go to the theatre.

D Write.

1   make / cakes / we / great

   We make great cakes.

2   they / oranges / eat

   _____

3   play / you / snow / in / the

   _____

4   the / watch / they / TV / in / bedroom

   _____

E Listen and number.

☐   ☐   ☐

☐   1   ☐

F Say.

I love Friday and Saturday. On Friday I ride my bike. On Saturday I watch TV.

buy   ride   play   make   watch   swim

11 I'm from Paris.

Lesson 3

crisps   maths   popcorn   scooter

English
like
live
at the weekend

A Read.

Email

New   Reply   Forward   Print   Delete   Send & Receive

Hi!

My name is John. I'm nine years old and I'm from Paris. I haven't got any brothers or sisters, but I've got lots of friends. I live with my mum.

On Friday Mum and I go to the cinema. I eat popcorn. Mum doesn't like popcorn. She eats crisps.

At the weekend I ride my scooter in the park. I don't like bikes.

My school is cool. I like maths, but I don't like English.

Bye for now!

John

B Circle.

1 John has got brothers / (friends.)
2 On Friday John goes to the park / cinema.
3 Mum doesn't like crisps / popcorn.
4 At the weekend John rides his bike / scooter.
5 He likes maths / English.

C Look and learn.

Mr Fry doesn't like my drawing.

I/you/we/they don't swim
he/she/it doesn't swim

don't = do not
doesn't = does not

We don't like popcorn.

D Write don't or doesn't.

1 I _____don't_____ eat crisps.

2 You _____ play tennis on Friday.

3 They _____ like chocolate.

4 Jack _____ ride a scooter.

5 We _____ have a maths lesson today.

6 Lynn _____ cook.

E Say.

I like skateboards.
I don't like scooters.

He likes skateboards.
He doesn't like scooters.

F Write.

Email

Hi!

My name is _____.

At the weekend I _____
_____.

I like _____.

I don't like _____.

Bye for now!

_____

109

cave dragonfly goat island panda sun moon

A Listen and read.

B Look and learn.

Do you like goats?

No, I don't.

Do I play ...?
Yes, I do.
No, I don't.

Do you play ...?
Yes, you do.
No, you don't.

Does he/she/it play ...?
Yes, he/she/it does.
No, he/she/it doesn't.

Does she eat carrots?
Yes, she does.

Do we play ...?
Yes, we do.
No, we don't.

Do you play ...?
Yes, you do.
No, you don't.

Do they play ...?
Yes, they do.
No, they don't.

Do they live in a castle?
No, they don't.

C Write.

1 Does your friend work?   No, he ___doesn't___ .
2 Do you live in a cave?   No, I _____ .
3 Does a lizard eat insects?   Yes, it _____ .
4 Do you love parties?   Yes, we _____ .
5 Does she play tennis?   No, she _____ .

D Listen and tick (✔).

1

2

3

4

E Say.

Do you like school?

Yes, I do. Do you like popcorn?

No, I don't.

morning   afternoon   night   laugh   go to bed   study

A Listen and read.

lucky
at ... o'clock

These children are friends. What do they do every day? They get up at 8 o'clock. They eat breakfast and they go to the beach. They play in the morning. They play in the afternoon! They're happy and they laugh a lot.

Look! That's Gary. He's wearing a yellow T-shirt. What does he do? He has fun with his friends.

At night he watches TV. He doesn't study. He goes to bed at 10 o'clock. Lucky Gary!

B Match.

1   These children are   at 8 o'clock.
2   They get up   to the beach.
3   They go   at 10 o'clock.
4   Gary has   friends.
5   Gary goes to bed   fun with his friends.

C Look and learn.

What do you do every day?

We play in the park!

What do I/you/we/they do ...?
What does he/she/it do ...?

every day
in the morning
in the afternoon
at night
at 8 o'clock

What do you do at 7 o'clock?
I eat breakfast.

D Circle.

1 What do / **does** he do every day?
2 What do you do in / **at** the morning?
3 What does we / **he** do at 6 o'clock?
4 What do / does they do in the afternoon?
5 What does Anna do in / **at** night?

Say it!

Listen and say.
look
afternoon

Read and listen.
Look at that kangaroo on his cool scooter.

E Sing.

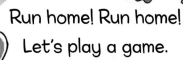

Get up! Get up!
Sleepy head!
Get up! Get up!
Jump out of bed!

Run home! Run home!
Let's play a game.
Run home! Run home!
Let's climb a tree.

Eat your breakfast.
Eat it all!
Eat your breakfast.
Go to school!

Go to bed.
Go to bed.
Sleepy head.
Go to bed.

12 It's our favourite season.

 spring summer autumn winter hot cold

favourite holiday season

Do you like our poster?

A Read.

Spring

The trees are green. What are those? They're beautiful flowers.

Summer

It's our favourite season. We're on holiday! Where do we go? We go to the island and we swim in the sea. We go to the mountains too.

Autumn

We go to school. Who do we see? All our friends! Everybody is happy. We play and we study.

Winter

Now it isn't hot. It's cold! When do we have a party? At New Year!

B Circle.

 1

 2

 3

 4

1 They're beautiful (flowers) / trees.
2 We go to the mountain / island.

3 We're in school / on holiday.
4 We like autumn / summer.

C Look and learn.

When are the holidays?

Today! Hooray!

What?	flower
Where?	in the house
When?	at night
Who?	grandma

Who is that?
My teacher.

D Write Who, What, Where or When.

1 _____What_____ is your favourite season?   Autumn.
2 _____ is that boy?   My brother.
3 _____ is your house?   In London.
4 _____ do you study?   In the afternoon.

E Say.

Who is your best friend?

Lucas.

When do you get up at the weekend?

At 10 o'clock.

What is your favourite season?

Autumn.

Where do you live?

In London.

F Draw and write.

My best friend's name is
_____. _____ gets
up _____ at the
weekend. _____ favourite
season is _____.
_____ lives in _____.

115

Let's remember!

A Find and stick.

goat   crisps   scooter   dragonfly   castle   cheese

B Write.

autumn   bedroom   ~~Friday~~   kitchen   living room
spring   Sunday   Wednesday   winter

Days	Seasons	House
Friday		

C Circle.

1 It's a nice night. The sun / (moon) is beautiful.
2 Who / What is that woman? My teacher.
3 It's hot / cold in the summer.
4 When do you eat basket / breakfast at the weekend?
5 What's your favourite / lucky food?
6 Sweets / Cakes haven't got any flour.

116

D Circle.

1 There are some glass / glasses in the kitchen.
2 Oh no! I haven't got some / any milk!
3 Have you got some / any oranges?
4 There are three men / man in the boat.
5 What's in the bag? Five potato / potatoes.
6 There are some / any nice beaches on the island.

E Match.

Where is Mr Green?

He's next to his car.

He's in his car.

He's under his car.

He's behind his car.

He's on his car.

He's in front of his car.

F Write.

1 They _____love_____ (love) spring.
2 Tim _____ (not ride) his scooter in winter.
3 _____ you _____ (study) in the afternoon?
4 Do you live in a big house? No, I _____ .
5 She _____ (go) to bed at 10 o'clock.
6 Where _____ Emily _____ (work)?

117

Fun and Games

It's summer. Tina and Jim are on holiday with their family. They're looking at a Beluga whale. These whales are white.

Quiz time!

Are whales fish?
a Yes, they are.
b No, they aren't.

A Match.

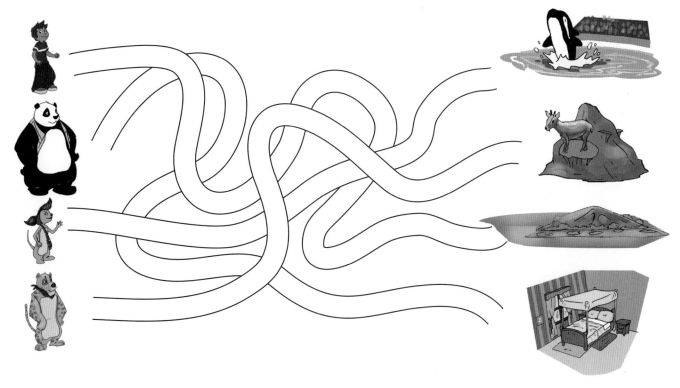

B Chant.

H-O-L-I-D-A-Y

We love holidays.
Come on everybody!
Let's go on holiday.

Chocolate, sweets and popcorn too.
Holiday food,
For me and you!

Go summer! Go summer!
Everybody say!
Go summer! Go summer!
Hooray!

C Make.

1

2

5

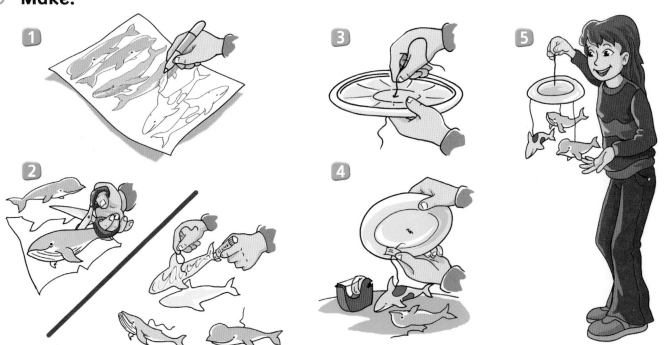

119

Little Red Riding Hood

This story is from Germany.

Mum   Little Red Riding Hood   The wolf

1

The apples are for Grandma.

Six red apples! A birthday present for Grandma! Goodbye, Mum!

Bye. Be careful!

2

Hello, small rabbits. Hello, small birds!

Hello, Little Red Riding Hood.

3

The big bad wolf!

Oh no!

Hello. What are those?

They're apples for Grandma.

4

Is Grandma nice?

Yes, she is. These flowers are for Grandma.

Bye!

5

Hello, Grandma. It's Little Red Riding Hood.

6

A wolf?

Grandma?

Grandma

The hunter

mouth

story

bad

Let's sing!

121

122

The bird

The fox

The rabbit

slow fast race sleep walk

stop

Let's sing!

Wonderful World 1 Pupil's Book

Jennifer Heath

Publisher: Jason Mann

Director of Content Development: Sarah Bideleux

Commissioning Editor: Carol Goodwright

Development Editor: Lynn Thomson

Assistant Editor: Manuela Barros

Content Project Editor: Amy Smith

Art Director: Natasa Arsenidou

Cover Designer: Vasiliki Christoforidou

Text Designers: Tania Diakaki, Sophia Ioannidou

Compositor: Sophia Ioannidou

National Geographic Editorial Liaison: Leila Hishmeh

Acknowledgements

Illustrated by Panagiotis Angeletakis and Theodoros Piakis

Song Credits: Music composed by Evdoxia Banani and Vagelis Markantonis

Recorded at Motivation Sound Studios and GFS-PRO Studio

Production at GFS-PRO Studio by George Flamouridis

The publisher would like to thank the following sources for permission to adapt and reproduce their copyright protected material:
Bondi Beach Public School for information in Unit 4 Lesson 1 and Unit 5 Lesson 1. More information about the school can be found on the website: www.bondibeach-p.schools.nsw.edu.au/

The publisher would like to thank the following sources for permission to reproduce their copyright protected photos:
Corbis - p. 29 (Graham Oliver/Juice Images); **Istockphoto** - pp. 34 (happyborder), 45 (alxpin, Leslie Banks), 94 (Sean Prior); **National Geographic** - pp. 34 (Robert Clark), 40 (Matthias Klum), 58 (Annie Griffiths), 64 (B. Anthony Stewart), 70 (Annie Griffiths), 76 (Karen Kasmauski), 82 (Tomasz Tomaszewsk), 88 (Justin Guariglia), 100 (Tim Laman), 106 (David Arnold), 112 (James P. Blair), 118 (Tim Laman); **Photolibrary Group**, p. 33 (Fancy); **Photos.com** - pp. 52, 89l, 89r; **Shutterstock** - pp.30 (Glenda M. Powers), (Kamira), 42 (Christian Musat, Pichugin Dmitry, Schalke fotografie/Melissa Schalke, silver-john, Ian Scott, Paul Banton, John Carnemolla, Anna Jurkovska), 45 (Nastya22, eale Cousland, Artush) 54 (Sheldunov Andrew), 60 (Monkey Business Images, Larisa Lofitskaya, Thomas M Perkins, Muellek Josef, 65 (Kiselev Andrey Valerevich), 84 (Len Green, Thomas M Perkins, Nagy-Bagoly Arpad, WAMVD), 90 (wildarrow, jan kranendonk, Stephen Finn, David Iliff, Kurhan), 100 (matka_Wariatka), 102 (Monkey Business Images), 108 (Tamakiik, Catalin Petolea), 114 (Monkey Business Images, Iakov Kalinin, Kelly Young, danilo ducak, Doug Baines).

© 2012 National Geographic Learning, as part of Cengage Learning

ISBN: 978-1-111-40064-4

National Geographic Learning
Cheriton House
North Way
Andover
Hampshire
SP10 5BE
United Kingdom

Cengage Learning is a leading provider of customized learning solutions with office locations around the globe, including Singapore, the United Kingdom, Australia, Mexico, Brazil and Japan. Locate your local office at:
international.cengage.com/region

Cengage Learning products are represented in Canada by Nelson Education, Ltd.

Visit National Geographic Learning online at
ngl.cengage.com
Visit our corporate website at **www.cengage.com**

Printed in China by RR Donnelley
Print Number: 13 Print Year: 2019